AF886583

How To Cope With Separation

Useful Information That May Be Helpful For You

Brent Bowyer, Esq.

Jon M. Midtgard, Esq.

ISBN: 978-1-941645-63-5

Designed and Published by:

Speakeasy Publications
73-03 Bell Blvd, #10
Oakland Gardens, NY 11364

www.SpeakeasyMarketingInc.com

888-225-8594

DISCLAIMER

This publication is intended to be informational only. No legal advice is being given, and no attorney-client relationship is intended to be created by reading this material. If you are facing legal issues, whether criminal or civil, seek professional legal counsel to get your questions answered.

American Divorce Association for Men (ADAM)

Metro Detroit – Southfield
2000 Town Center, Suite 2350
Southfield MI 48075

(248) 356-2326

www.AdamDivorceLaw.com

TESTIMONIALS

"During my divorce, Jon Midtgard acted like I was part of his family. He took my matters to heart and really went the extra mile for me. Jon is very knowledgeable, extremely hard working, trustworthy, loyal, a great listener, and very compassionate. Jon was not only professional but also very empathetic and a great counselor. He was always reassuring me that everything was going well and I trusted him to take care of everything. I needed an attorney that was understanding but also assertive in getting the job done. After hiring Jon, I could rest and feel at ease during the process of my divorce/child custody case. I would highly recommend Jon to anybody who needs a strong, intelligent, hardworking, trustworthy attorney that will go the extra mile for men's rights." ***- Andy B.***

"I just wanted to send you a note of thanks concerning Brent Bowyer and his staff during my recent divorce. I came to your offices to file for divorce, pretty much ignorant of the whole process. I was assigned to Brent, and in just a few minutes he was able to settle my nerves and lay out the groundwork for what was to come. At the end of the first meeting the complaint was prepared and ready to be filed. As the legal process kicked in, I was faced with a lot of questions (due mostly to my own ignorance) and decision making. Even when Brent was in court, his legal assistant took my calls. She made sure that Brent addressed all of my questions and concerns promptly and efficiently. After all is said and done, your firm took what I thought would be the most difficult event I had ever been through and made it an almost easy process." ***- Tim G.***

"Thanks Jon. You are in my opinion, one of the best, honest, and straight forward attorneys I know. I have passed your name on to a number of other friends and associates for obvious reasons."

- Larry M.

"All is going well so far with both me and the boys. They are accepting this rather well under the circumstances. I am still involved in their lives with all of their activities. Their mother seems to look rather tired and haggard lately. I think that her new life has really dealt her a bad hand of cards so to speak. Financially, I'm feeling the sting of a scaled down lifestyle, but as long as I can keep my home I'll be grateful. I hope that all has been well with you. I really enjoyed working with you and every time I hear a commercial on the radio for ADAM, I think about you with a smile on my face and in my heart. I appreciate everything you've done for me and I'll never forget you."

- James T.

Table Of Contents

About The Authors

Attorney Brent Bowyer

Brent Bowyer is a co-owner and partner of the law firm Bowyer and Midtgard, P.C., practicing family law exclusively. Mr. Bowyer earned his B.B.A. from Western Michigan University and his J.D. degree from The John Marshall Law School in Chicago, Ill. He is admitted to the Michigan Supreme Court, Federal District Court, and the U.S. Supreme Court. Mr. Bowyer is a member of the Family Law Section of the State Bar of Michigan, and the Oakland and Wayne County Bar Associations.

Mr. Bowyer has practiced family law exclusively since 1996, litigating hundreds of divorce cases in that time. He has been a repeat guest on the Hardcore Mortgage and Business Show on 97.1 FM talk radio, and has been quoted as an expert in many news media articles including Metro Parent Detroit Magazine. He has also been a guest speaker on the national Fox News Network, and is a frequent speaker at the State Bar of Michigan Family Law Section Mid-Winter Seminars.

Attorney Jon M. Midtgard

Jon M. Midtgard is a co-owner and partner of the law firm Bowyer and Midtgard, P.C. Mr. Midtgard graduated from James Madison College at Michigan State University with honors and the Detroit College of Law; a recipient of a jurisprudence achievement award. Mr. Midtgard is admitted to the State Bar of Michigan and Federal District Court. He has practiced family law exclusively since 1996, and has litigated hundreds of divorce cases in that time.

Jon is a member of the Family Law Section of the State Bar of Michigan, as well as the Oakland County Bar Association for which he has served on the Family Court Committee, American Inns of Court, Law Day Committee, and has participated in Bench/Bar conferences relative to family law. He is also a frequent speaker on family law topics for the Institute of Continuing Legal Education and a member of the Michigan Inter-Professional Association. Jon was a recent guest on the Michigan syndicated news talk radio show, WJIM AM 1240 with Michael Patrick Shiels. He is a repeat guest on the Hardcore Mortgage and Business Show on 97.1 FM, and he was a commentator on 'Due Process' WDIV Channel 4 Detroit.

What Is Permanent Separation And Legal Separation?

Parties may agree to live apart, or may even be living apart for years and still be married. There is no permanent separation in Michigan. However, parties can do what is called "legal separation." Michigan's version of legal separation is called a Judgment of Separation.

How Is Legal Separation Determined In Michigan?

This is a legal action filed in the same manner as a divorce, and through the same court system as a divorce. The Judgment would set forth a binding allocation of assets and liabilities and establish custody, parenting time and support.

A legal separation case is similar to a divorce case in every way. However, at the end of the process, the parties are still legally married. Should either wish to be divorced in the future, he or she would have to file a Complaint for Divorce and wait the requisite waiting period to complete that process. If the Judgment of Separate Maintenance is done correctly, assets and debt accumulated thereafter would not be divisible in a subsequent divorce.

Whether parties are legally separated or not, the issues of custody, parenting time, and support for minor children are always modifiable based upon a showing of a change of circumstances.

Legal separation will be done typically for unique purposes, and it is the exception, not the rule. One reason someone would seek a legal separation instead of a divorce is if, for religious reasons, they're not allowed to divorce or they do not believe in divorce. They can then separate from their spouse in every way and would address all issues through a court case, and in the end be legally separated instead of divorced.

The start of a legal separation case would be to file a Complaint for Separate Maintenance. This case will then address all issues including custody, parenting time, and child support if there are minor children. The court would also have jurisdiction over any and all property and debts and spousal support. The end result is that you are still legally married to your spouse but you are separated in every way, including responsibility for debts and division of assets. Legal separation can only be done by agreement, and if one party wants to divorce instead, they have an absolute right to do so.

How Is Legal Separation Different From Dissolution Of Marriage?

A Judgment of Separate Maintenance and Judgment of Divorce are essentially the same. The main difference is that the parties remain legally married after entry of a Judgment of Separate Maintenance and would have to file a divorce down the road.

Separate Maintenance actions are typically filed when the parties believe there may be a chance for reconciliation down the road or where they may have religious or philosophic objection to divorce. Separate maintenance actions may also be filed for estate planning purposes, or in order to allow a spouse to remain on the other spouse's health insurance after the parties separate. This last issue of health insurance can be complicated. If you are considering a legal separation to keep health insurance in place, you should first find out if this will work with your specific health insurance plan.

Does A Legal Separation Protect Someone From The Debts Of Their Spouse?

Filing for and completing a legal separation through the court system will protect you from the debts of your spouse. A properly drafted Judgment of Separate Maintenance would typically divide debts accumulated as of that time and provide that debts incurred thereafter would be the responsibility of the party incurring them.

However, just as in the case of a divorce, a Judgment of Separate Maintenance is not binding on a creditor. So if a spouse is a co-signor to his or her spouse's debt, the creditor can still enforce it, and failure to pay the debt would still hurt the co-signer's credit. This is why it is crucial to run a credit report to ensure that all debts are being accounted for in the Judgment.

If a party is assuming joint debt, that party should be required to pay it off or refinance it as soon as possible. Further, appropriate remedies should be included in the Judgment if the party that assumed a joint debt default or fail to make timely payments. This could include the ability of the other party to seek alimony from the party that failed to pay a joint debt.

At the completion of the legal separation case and entry of the judgment of separate maintenance, you and your spouse will be legally separated in every way. Your assets will be separate, and your debts will be separate. You will no longer be responsible for your spouse's bills or expenses.

Does Someone Need To Go To The Court To Legally Separate From Their Spouse?

Yes. You are required to go through the court system to have a legal separation completed. A Complaint for Separate Maintenance is filed in the county through the Circuit Court in which one of the parties has resided for more than 10 days. The process is essentially the same as a divorce lawsuit and is filed as a Complaint for Separate Maintenance, except that at the end of the process the parties are formally separated, financially and otherwise, but still technically married. A legal separation involves the same process as a divorce case in every way including amount of time and issues addressed, and cost.

What Are The Benefits Of Legal Separation Vs Divorce?

Health insurance for the children would still be available in most situations after legal separation has been completed. One benefit of legal separation is the continuation of health insurance benefits for the spouse. This is the exact reason why some people choose to do a Judgment of Separate Maintenance instead of a Judgment of Divorce.

As to the spouse, it would depend on the eligibility requirements of the health insurance provider. This could be problematic if the parties don't follow the rules, as the employer or the insurance provider could deem the continuation of benefits fraudulent and threaten legal action against the policyholder, including but not limited to employment termination or prosecution.

Whether the health insurance coverage will continue for your spouse after a Judgment of Separate Maintenance depends on your specific health insurance plan. Before going forward with a Complaint for Separate Maintenance for the sole purpose of continuing health insurance coverage, the attorney would want to know that your health insurance is going to continue coverage.

In a divorce matter, health insurance coverage terminates automatically at the completion of divorce and entry of the final Judgment of Divorce. If your spouse is currently on your health insurance, that will not continue after the divorce.

Legal separation, also known as a Judgment of Separate Maintenance, is better than simply living apart without the benefit of a court order. The Court Order would create enforceable rights as to custody, parenting time, support and property division.

Further, the Court Order would separate the parties' assets and liabilities as of the date of the Judgment and allow the parties to operate without fear that they would have to share assets or debts accumulated while they are separated.

What Reasons Lead People To Decide To Pursue A Legal Separation Versus A Divorce?

Parties would typically choose legal separation if there is a reasonable chance they may reconcile and would want to avoid having to remarry should that happen. They also may have a religious or philosophical opposition to divorce but still want to arrange their finances and custody issues to recognize that they are no longer living together.

Legal separation allows the parties to separate all of their affairs and to basically live completely separate lives while still being legally married. This is a valid reason to consider filing for legal separation, and will protect you from any future claims by your spouse or concerns about liability for his or her debts in the future. It will also insulate you from any future claims your spouse would have against your assets. These estate planning issues would make a Judgment of Separate Maintenance preferable to a divorce.

Some parties may choose legal separation with the idea that the party who would otherwise lose health insurance upon a divorce may still be eligible if there were a Judgment of Separate Maintenance. If you currently are on your spouse's health insurance policy, getting divorced will terminate that coverage automatically. One strategy is to stay married but to do a separation agreement.

Most health insurance providers will continue to allow coverage under these circumstances. However, you should check with your health insurance provider to confirm that health insurance coverage following entry of the Judgment of Separate Maintenance will, in fact, continue.

MISCONCEPTIONS ABOUT SEPARATION WITHIN A MARRIAGE

The two biggest misconceptions are that separating can be considered "abandonment" or that the court will treat a separation the same as a divorce in determining property settlement or support.

Married men often believe that if they move out and begin living separately, they have started some sort of separation as defined under the law. It's common to believe that this starts a legal process or is required prior to filing for divorce. However, that is not the case. Abandonment is an outdated, common law term wherein a man could be charged with a crime for leaving his wife and children without any means of support. It would rarely, if ever, be charged today.

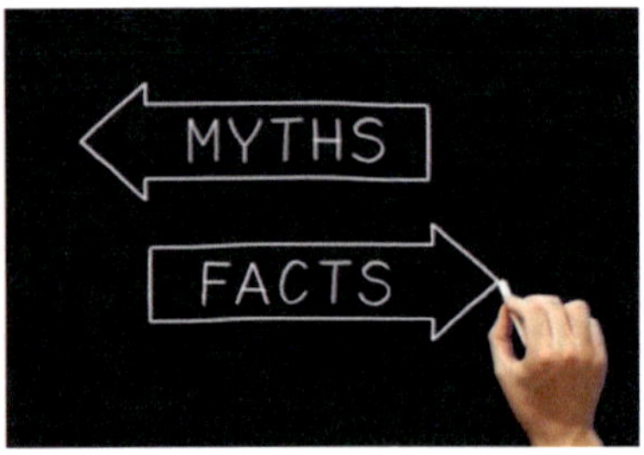

Under Michigan law, living apart from your spouse has really no ground rules and no special laws that apply. You are in a precarious scenario where you must trust each other and trust what is happening day to day with respect to the bills, your children, and your property.

The issue with leaving the home without making arrangements for custody, parenting time, support, payment of bills, and disposition of assets, including the home, is that the person moving out loses control of the situation. Leaving the home and the children with the other parent could create a custodial environment, and as such, make it difficult for the parent who is moving out to seek custody in the future. Should the parent that remains with the children refuse to allow parenting time, it could take several weeks or longer to start a divorce and obtain a hearing to get that parenting time.

As to assets, liabilities, and support, people frequently assume that the court will treat them as if they are divorced when they separate. In fact, Michigan law is clear that you are divorced only when a formal divorce is granted and, as such, any assets and liabilities accumulated between the date of separation and divorce could potentially be divided at the time of divorce. In Michigan, you can file for divorce or file for legal separation.

While separation may be factored in to how assets or debts are to be divided, that isn't guaranteed. Likewise, in an alimony case the court can look at the entire length of the actual marriage rather than just the time the parties resided together.

In addition to divorce and legal separation, a third option for a very limited few is filing for an annulment.

Filing for legal separation has nothing to do with moving out at the beginning stages of divorce. Living separately at the beginning stages of divorce is something that may or may not be appropriate for your specific situation. You might file a Complaint for Divorce, a Complaint for Separate Maintenance, or in a very unlikely scenario, a Complaint for Annulment. At the same time, you might be living together, apart, or planning on moving out.

Choosing to live apart is not a "legal separation" under Michigan law. That just becomes a husband and wife that no longer live in the same house and do not yet have a divorce case filed. Michigan does not require parties to live separately prior to filing divorce like some states do. In Michigan, you file for divorce and then you may live together during the entire divorce process, part of the divorce process, or you may not live together at all. In fact, some people have been living apart for years before they file for divorce.

Trial Separation Or Legal Separation?

In Michigan, there is no formal trial separation, nor is there any requirement that the parties live apart for any length of time in order to get divorced. The only requirement is a 60 day waiting period between filing for a divorce and entry of a Judgment when the parties don't have minor children and a 180 day waiting period when minor children are involved.

In a case where parties are seeking to shorten the 180 day waiting period, the Court may consider that the parties were separated for some period prior to filing divorce. In no event can a divorce be granted in less than 60 days from when it was filed.

Parties may choose to live apart with one of the parties agreeing to move out of the house at the beginning of a divorce, and this may be seen as temporary. There really are no laws or a specific legal process to use as a guide.

There is no case that would be filed with the court involving a trial separation. If the parties can reach agreement with regards to living separately on a trial basis, advice from an experienced divorce attorney prior to making final decisions regarding such a living arrangement would be beneficial.

The primary concern in separating without the benefit of a court order is that the parties lack the ability to enforce agreements they may have reached as to custody, parenting time, support, or disposition of assets.

It is advisable to file a Complaint for Divorce or a Complaint for Separate Maintenance and enter into consent orders which would provide recourse should the other party violate an agreement.

DIVORCING AFTER SEPARATION AND GETTING HELP FROM AN ATTORNEY

An experienced divorce and family law attorney can ensure that all laws and procedures are followed properly in your separation. You will need assistance for everything from filing the paperwork, attending the court date, to drafting the final Judgment of Separate Maintenance.

The legal advice to separate along with the benefit of a court order can be crucial in protecting a client's interests in custody, parenting time, support, property, and debt division. Pursuing these issues through the court involves filing a lawsuit in the circuit court in the county where the parties reside. It is always advisable to have a lawsuit filed and processed by an experienced attorney.

Court personnel are not allowed to give legal advice, and parties representing themselves are held to the same standards on procedure and substantive law as if they had an attorney. Unrepresented or poorly represented parties will inevitably spend a lot of time spinning their wheels trying to figure out how to proceed with the lawsuit.

When it comes to drafting the final agreement and order, it is crucial to include all potential issues and ensure that there are no loose ends. The point of a Judgment of Separate Maintenance is to create enforceability of the parties' agreement and to have a binding Judgment should the parties later divorce. It must be handled correctly in order to ensure that this happens.

Without an attorney, there's no way to be certain that the agreement that you have made is properly drafted and will be enforceable. There is no way of protecting your rights without having an attorney prepare the documents and control the procedures in your case.

If A Couple Decides To Divorce After A Period Of Legal Separation, Is The Divorce Handled Any Differently Than A Regular Divorce?

Yes, the divorce is handled differently in this situation. There would still be a 60 day minimum waiting period between the filing of the divorce and entry of a divorce judgment. If your divorce is done following legal separation, it will make the divorce case much simpler. At that point there are no property or debts to be in dispute. Essentially, if there are no issues to litigate in the divorce case, the case would be over very quickly and painlessly.

Even if you are dealing with a difficult person, there is very little that person can do to prevent you from getting the divorce completed in a timely manner. A divorce following a legal separation is a very simple process to complete.

More importantly, a properly drafted Judgment of Separate Maintenance will greatly reduce, if not eliminate, any disputes over issues between the parties, as those would have been disposed of in the Judgment of Separate Maintenance and binding upon the parties in the divorce.

In cases with children, where that waiting period is normally 6 months, a Judgment of Separate Maintenance should, but won't necessarily, provide grounds for the divorce judge to expedite the process.

Issues of custody, parenting time, and support of minor children are always modifiable upon a showing of a change of circumstances, but the Judgment of Separate Maintenance would provide guidance for the Court on these issues and would normally be enforced.

Division of assets and debt as set forth in the Judgment of Separate Maintenance would be incorporated by reference in the divorce action and would be non-modifiable and enforceable.

How Does Separation Affect Property Rights, Custody Rights?

Separation can, but won't necessarily, affect the property division in a subsequent divorce. Michigan is an equitable distribution of property state which means the court applies certain factors in allocating assets and debt regardless of the parties living apart before or at any point during the divorce process.

One of those factors is the contribution by each party to the accumulation of assets and, as such, assets or debt that was accumulated post-separation could be primarily awarded to the party who earned them. The bottom line is that remaining married while separated puts any assets you have at risk and may make you liable for debts your spouse is incurring as well as a longer term of alimony than if you had divorced at the time of separation.

Living apart without the protection of a custody order is leaves you no way to enforce parenting time. It will certainly affect your custody rights if you are living apart from your children. The police typically won't assist you without a court order, which results in custody being dictated by the party who is in possession of the children. Further, the longer the person moving out is on the outside looking in so to speak, the more likely it is that the court will award custody to the parent with whom the children reside.

It can also affect issues involving personal property, and can trigger child support or spousal support to be paid. If you move out of the marital home, you may lose any control of what's happening at the home on a day to day basis, and you may also lose control over any valuables or personal property at that home. If you leave, your spouse could destroy, remove, or try to hide property from you. Therefore, moving out of the home is something that needs to be done when both parties can trust each other and both parties feel they have a valid agreement. There needs to be a meaningful discussion prior to vacating the home, and ideally this agreement should be a written agreement.

If parties find it necessary to separate, it is advisable to file a Complaint for Divorce or Complaint for Separate Maintenance (legal separation) and obtain temporary court orders addressing custody, parenting time, support, payment of bills, and other financial matters before vacating or moving out of the house.

This allows for a temporary agreement to be made regarding whatever issues are relevant. If there are minor children, you can make a temporary agreement regarding custody, parenting time, child support, and payment of monthly bills prior to vacating the home. Even without children there can be temporary agreements regarding payment of monthly bills and other ground rules. You are always free to leave temporarily or go away for a few nights to keep the peace, or "give each other some space." But moving out with no plan and no agreement can cause devastating consequences.

If you are married and do not have minor (under eighteen years) children there still should be some understanding and agreement prior to moving out regarding issues of paying monthly bills. It is better to know prior to moving if you're responsible for all of the bills at the house or a large majority of those bills before committing yourself to rent and other expenses at a second home. Making an agreement regarding payment of monthly bills is commonly referred to as status quo. Please note that any written agreements made without a legal case filed will not be enforceable.

It is not normally possible for one party to have their spouse removed from the home, so the only way you would be leaving is if you voluntarily agree to leave. You are not required to move out and doing so should be done based on mutually agreeable terms and with a full discussion of what is expected of both parties prior to moving out. This is a common mistake that people make early on in a divorce case. Unless there is some sort of domestic violence happening, it is not possible to remove your spouse from their home.

Concerns That People Have Before Separation

The first concern is, "Can someone draft a separation agreement without a lawyer?" Yes, it is possible to draft a separation agreement without an attorney.

First of all, the best way to have an enforceable separation agreement is to enter a Judgment of Separate Maintenance with the court. Entering into an agreement for separation without a legal separation case filed first will not be enforceable. This includes an agreement that has been notarized. Having a document notarized simply means a Notary Public has concluded that the person signing it is who he says he is. It does not automatically make an invalid agreement enforceable.

The issue of doing this type of case with no attorney raises the same issues that are raised with any do-it-yourself approach to legal matters. Although there is no technical requirement that a party hire an attorney to file a Separate Maintenance action, you would be ill advised to proceed without one. A Complaint for Separate Maintenance is a lawsuit just like a divorce action and the court has strict and often complicated procedures that must be followed. Further, great care must be taken in the drafting of the Judgment to ensure that it covers all issues and that it will be enforced down the road, including but not limited to in a subsequent divorce action.

Is Legal Separation Required Before A Divorce Can Be Granted?

No. You're not required to file a legal separation before a divorce can be granted. In Michigan divorce and legal separation actually are two different things. These two options have their pros and cons, and making an educated choice as to which one to pursue is an important decision. However, a legal separation is not required prior to filing for a divorce.

Is It Possible For The Wife To Get Support From Her Husband During A Separation?

Even when a divorce has not been filed, child support or spousal support (alimony) can be obtained after separation by filing a Complaint for Child Support, a Complaint for Custody, or a Complaint for Separate Maintenance.

If you have minor children, support can be ordered in the form of child support and maintenance of status quo on monthly bills.

When there are no minor children it is still possible for you to be required to continue to pay monthly expenses on behalf of your wife or be required to pay temporary spousal support based on the 12 factors under Michigan law for determining spousal support.

There are many factors to be considered when determining whether you will be responsible to pay support to your spouse. The primary factor would involve looking at status quo and who has been paying the bills in the past. The primary factors for consideration are the income of the husband and the wife and the monthly bills.

HOW CAN AN ATTORNEY HELP WITH TEMPORARY ORDERS IN FAMILY COURT?

Temporary orders are typically entered in family law cases while the matter is pending in court but prior to the final order completing the case. The orders dictate the terms of what the parties are required to follow during the litigation. These orders can address financial and custody issues while the matter is pending, including temporary custody, parenting time or support, and payment of bills. The orders may also issue a restraining order preventing either party from engaging in secret or improper transfers of assets, changes to bank accounts or beneficiaries on life insurance, changing health insurance coverage, or any other changes to financial matters while the case is being litigated. This gives both parties some security that there will not be any changes made except those done by agreement.

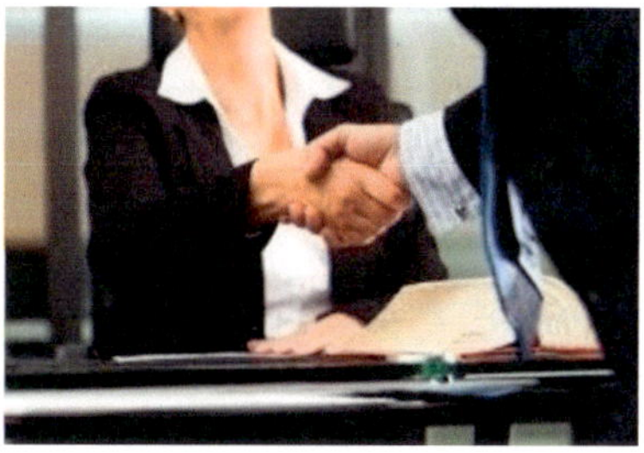

One reason to file a lawsuit before the other party does is so that temporary order(s) can be entered which include terms to your advantage. These orders are entered ex-parte (without a hearing) based upon what was alleged in the initial complaint for divorce, custody, or separate maintenance. The attorney would rather submit their own version of these orders than to have their clients be on the receiving end of whatever the other side has convinced the judge to sign.

If there are minor children in a divorce matter, the temporary order can dictate what will happen with custody, parenting time, and child support issues. These temporary orders continue in enforcement through to the end of the divorce or separation case. The temporary order is done to give peace of mind to one or both of the parties to dictate the terms of their temporary agreements on various issues.

Other temporary orders can be entered by agreement (stipulation) of the parties or as a result of a motion hearing addressing these types of issues.

Regardless of how the orders are completed and signed by the court, the terms can intimately affect your life and must be handled properly.

How Does A Lawyer Help With A Temporary Order? Are They Always Necessary?

Your lawyer helps with a temporary order by discussing the terms of this order and by having the order written. Some type of temporary order is almost always necessary in a divorce or separation matter. Temporary orders can address financial issues including status quo and payment of monthly bills. They can also address issues involving minor children such as custody, parenting time, and child support. It is always good practice to have a temporary order in place to validate any agreements that the parties have made in their case.

Attorneys maintain that at a minimum, an ex parte mutual asset restraining order is necessary in all cases. This order basically puts the parties on notice that they cannot engage in out of the ordinary financial transactions such as selling or hiding assets, changing beneficiaries on insurance and investments, emptying the bank account or running up extraordinary credit card debt.

A significant part of family law litigation involves entering other temporary orders to prevent a financial or custody situation from getting worse. For instance, if a party is denying or limiting parenting time to an unacceptable level, it is crucial to get that fixed in court rather than waiting the length of the case and setting a precedent that would be difficult to overcome at trial. Likewise, bills need to be paid and assets need to be protected while the litigation is pending. If these issues are not addressed, there would be catastrophic financial consequences for the family.

An attorney can seek entry of temporary orders at the outset of the case or by filing a motion and giving the other party 7 to 9 days advance notice of a court hearing wherein these issues would be decided.

WHAT IS MEDIATION?

Mediation is a non-binding settlement discussion. This is referred to as an alternative dispute resolution, meaning it is a way for the parties to meet with a third party and reach an agreement as opposed to conducting an expensive and drawn out trial.

Typically, a third party attorney is selected by the parties' attorneys or appointed by the judge to help settle the case. Each party's attorney would submit a written summary of the facts and law associated with the case as well as his or her suggestion on how the issues should be resolved. The mediator would review those summaries in advance and then schedule a mediation conference in which all parties and their attorneys would attend. The parties would either meet in the same room, or the mediator would go from office to office getting each side's position on the facts and law involved.

The mediator would attempt to reach an agreement by informing the parties how the law typically works and what he or she believes the judge is likely to do. In cases where the parties still cannot reach an agreement, it is common for the mediator to issue a recommendation on how the case should be resolved.

Mediation (as opposed to arbitration) is non-binding, meaning the mediator's recommendations are just a suggestion which the parties can follow or not. The next step after an unsuccessful mediation would be to go to trial.

If mediation is successful, it is common for the settlement of the parties to either be typed out and signed or recorded so as to make that settlement binding. This is done so that neither party can change his or her mind down the road. The purpose of this is to bring finality to the matter.

Any statements or settlement discussions made in conjunction with mediation are confidential and cannot be disclosed to the judge, unless a binding mediation agreement is reached. Otherwise, the only thing a judge could be told is that a party refused to attend or participate in good faith in spite of being ordered to do so.

When Is Mediation Appropriate?

Mediation is appropriate in most cases where the parties cannot reach an agreement on their own or with the help of their respective attorneys. Moreover, most judges require the parties to attempt mediation prior to conducting a trial in the matter.

There are some cases where mediation would not be appropriate and would require the judge to authorize mediation. The main reason for this would be where domestic violence has occurred or has been alleged. A hearing would have to be held, and the judge in the case would determine if mediation can take place in a safe and productive manner.

Does The A.D.A.M Law Office Get Involved In Mediations?

Yes. Mediation is fairly common in divorce or custody cases. All cases at A.D.A.M are started by ensuring the relevant facts are available and attempts are made to settle disputed issues with the other party's attorney. Should that fail, it is common to attempt mediation to bring the parties together and avoid trial.

An attorney is responsible for knowing all of the facts and issues associated with the case and to advocate on his or her client's behalf throughout the process. In the event mediation is successful, an attorney will ensure the mediation agreement addresses all issues and can be reduced to a Judgment of Divorce, legal separation, or custody order without further litigation.

How Does The Process Work? How Long Does Mediation Take?

Mediation can take place at the mediator's office, a conference room at the courthouse or at an attorney's office. A typical mediation will take 3 to 4 hours and be completed in one session. Particularly complicated or contentious cases could take a full day and even continue to several sessions.

What Makes A Case Too Complicated For Mediation?

Issues of domestic violence or other criminal behavior can complicate mediation. Cases where the parties cannot come to an agreement as to the verification and value of assets and liabilities can also

cause problems. It is common that mediation will be adjourned in order to obtain missing financial information. This includes cases in which parties are hiding, overvaluing, or undervaluing assets. Cases where a business or real estate needs to be valued also can complicate mediation, and attorneys are well advised to select mediators that understand issues of valuation to assist in bridging the gap.

Another issue that is difficult, if not impossible to mediate, is a request by either party to change the domicile, or state, in which the children are to live. This issue is extremely complicated and contentious, and is more like an "all or nothing" proposition. In cases where the judge is likely to grant a move, mediation may be appropriate to work out details of parenting time, transportation, and communication associated with such a move.

Not every situation is appropriate for mediation; however, giving strong consideration to such methods of alternate dispute resolution is always a good idea.

WHAT IS ANNULMENT AND HOW IS IT DIFFERENT FROM DIVORCE?

An annulment essentially means that the marriage was never legitimate, i.e. the parties are treated as if they were never properly married in the first place. A divorce involves a legally solemnized marriage that for one reason or another needs to be terminated.

There typically isn't a choice between which route to choose, as the grounds for an annulment are different from the grounds for a divorce. A divorce is granted if the court finds it has jurisdiction. It may also be granted if the court further finds that there has been a breakdown in the marital relationship to the extent that the objects of matrimony have been destroyed, that the parties can no longer remain together as husband and wife. An annulment is granted only when the court can conclude that the parties were never properly married in the first place.

Who Grants A Civil Annulment?

An annulment can be granted only by a family court judge in the county where one or both parties reside. It can only be granted after a hearing in front of a family court judge.

What Are The Most Common Reasons People Choose To Annul A Marriage?

Annulments can only be granted when the court concludes that the parties were never legitimately married in the first place. There are two situations where marriages can be annulled. These are when the marriage is void on its face or when a marriage is voidable based upon other circumstances.

A marriage is void on its face when either party or both parties lacked the capacity to enter into a marriage contract, and it is deemed never to have taken place because it was void from the beginning. Reasons for voiding a marriage include, but are not limited to, situations where the parties are related to one another by blood (siblings, first cousins, etc.), where one party is still married to someone else, where one party is a minor child without parental permission to marry, or where one party has been declared by a court as legally incompetent to enter into contracts on his or her own behalf.

If an action is voidable, the marriage is deemed valid until one of the parties brings an action to have it annulled. A marriage is voidable when one party can convince the court that the marriage was induced by fraud, coercion, or undue influence. Because marriage is a contract, the parties must mutually consent to enter into it. Thus, the proverbial "shotgun wedding," wherein the parties are forced to marry due to pregnancy or other circumstances under the threat of violence or prosecution is voidable because it was induced by coercion and was not voluntary.

Likewise, a situation where a woman has induced a man to marry her by falsely claiming she is pregnant can result in an annulment. If a party knowingly misrepresents her ability or willingness to have children, then the marriage could be annulled as the ability to have children is viewed as paramount in a marriage. Temporary lack of capacity at the time of the marriage ceremony, such as being under the influence of alcohol or drugs, so that free will is compromised, can also be grounds for an annulment.

Failure to disclose a lengthy criminal history to a prospective spouse could form the basis for an annulment whereas failure to be truthful to credit or wealth are generally not sufficient. There is a body of relatively complicated case law, statutes, and time limits governing these issues and therefore, consultation with an experienced attorney is necessary.

WHAT ARE THE STEPS AND PROCEDURES IN A CIVIL ANNULMENT?

A court must either find that the marriage is void on its face, because one or both parties lacked the capacity to marry, or else that the marriage is voidable due to other problems with the marriage contract.

What Is The General Timeline For A Civil Annulment?

Unlike a divorce, there is no waiting period that must elapse before the entry of a judgment of annulment. If a court can clearly determine that the marriage is void on its face, such as when one of the parties is still married, that annulment could be granted within a few weeks of when the action if filed.

In cases where the marriage is voidable, based upon arguments over the marriage contract, the process could continue for quite some time, including having the court conduct an evidentiary hearing (trial) to take testimony over disputed facts. In this case, the timeline of the case will depend upon the judge's schedule and ability to set aside sufficient time to conduct such a complicated hearing.

Parties are well advised to obtain an annulment in situations where the marriage is void so as to avoid any confusion if one of them wants to marry someone else, or as to government benefits, debtor creditor issues, and estate planning considerations. If a party discovers that he or she was still married to someone else when entering into the current marriage, the current marriage must be annulled to avoid being criminally charged with bigamy, or being married to more than one person at a time.

Annulments are preferred to divorces in that the parties are typically treated as if the marriage never occurred and would be restored to the position they were in at the time of the alleged marriage. Thus, individually held assets such as pensions, 401(k), real estate, and bank or investment accounts would not be subject to division in an annulment case unlike in a divorce where all assets of the parties are subject to division.

Other Advantages Of An Annulment Proceeding

Other advantages of an annulment proceeding would be:

A. To remove any stigma associated with having been divorced.

B. To start a subsequent marital relationship as if it is a first marriage.

C. To reinstate spousal support from a first marriage that would have otherwise been terminated due to the subsequent void or voidable marriage.

D. To reinstate pension, social security, or insurance benefits from a prior marriage that may have been terminated or suspended due to the subsequent void or voidable marriage.

E. There are no lengthy residency requirements like there are in a divorce proceeding.

F. There is no 60 day mandatory waiting period before there is a hearing.

Why Is It Important To Hire An Attorney When Seeking A Civil Annulment?

People regularly suggest that annulments and divorces are interchangeable. This is common when the parties wish to end their marriage very shortly after it has started. The length of the marriage is not a determining factor in obtaining an annulment. The determining factor is proving to the court that the marriage was void in the first place or that it is voidable due to other problems with the marriage contract. This is a fairly complicated argument to make and requires skill in the presentation of proof to the judge. Because of the difficulty in proving that voidable marriage can be annulled, a party may be advised to simply proceed with a divorce in short term marriages.

Furthermore, even if a marriage is annulled, there may need to be a division of jointly held assets and determination of custody, parenting time, and support for children the parties may have. Just as in a divorce or custody matter, these issues need to be handled with great care and expertise to ensure that the final order is in the children's best interest and will protect the client moving forward.

Made in the USA
Monee, IL
05 November 2026

67385057R00031